Bible Heroes— Cousins: Mary and Elizabeth

Read and Do Activities

by Mary E. Lysne

These stories are fun and easy to read.
A picture stands for a word.

STANDARD PUBLISHING
Cincinnati, Ohio

ISBN 0-7847-0101-6
The Standard Publishing Company, Cincinnati, Ohio.
A division of Standex International Corporation.
© 1993 by Mary E. Lysne
All rights reserved
Printed in the United States of America
23-02581

Angel News

A woman named 🧕 lived in Bible times. 🧕's husband was Z. 🧕 came from a 👪 of 👳s. So did Z. Z was a 👳. Z and 🧕 felt 😞. They wanted children. But 🧕 was old. She could not have children. Z and 🧕 prayed to God for a 👶. One day Z was in the temple. He was serving as 👳. Suddenly he saw an 👼. "Don't be afraid," the 👼 said. "God heard you pray. 🧕 will have a 👶 boy. You will name him John. He will be great." Z did not believe the 👼. "🧕 is too old," he said. "It will happen," the 👼 promised. "But you did not believe God's news. Now you will not be able to talk until the 👶 comes."

Adding Angels

God often used angels to bring good news. An angel brought good news to Elizabeth. Add up the angels on this page. How many can you find?

More Angel News

Z Zechariah | **Elizabeth** | **news** | **talk** | **hand** | **happy** | **baby** | **Mary** | **king**

Z left the temple. He went home to Elizabeth. What news Z had! Elizabeth wanted to hear the news. But Z could not talk. Maybe Z made hand signs. Maybe he wrote in the sand. But soon Elizabeth knew the angel's news. She believed the angel. How happy she was! Soon she became pregnant. Z and Elizabeth knew their baby would be very special. Later the angel came to another city. This time the news was for Mary. "God is happy with you," the angel said. "You will have a baby boy. He will be great. He will be king forever." Mary and Elizabeth were cousins. Their sons were cousins. God knew these cousins would change the world. And that is good news!

Picture Spelling

Every letter has a picture that takes its place. If you spell DOG it looks like 🐕○🌱. The pictures in the big box spell something. Can you figure out what they spell?

You Too?

angel | Mary | baby | God | Spirit | Elizabeth | love | mountain | shout

An angel promised Mary, "You will have a son." "I am not married. How can this happen?" Mary asked. "Your baby will be God's Son. God's Holy Spirit will make it happen. And listen to this — your cousin Elizabeth will have a baby too! God can do anything." What a surprise! Mary loved God. She obeyed God. "I will do what God wants," Mary said. She believed the angel's promise. Mary had many things to think about. So she went to the mountains. Elizabeth lived in the mountains. When Mary got there she shouted hello to Elizabeth. Right then the Holy Spirit filled Elizabeth and told her about Mary's baby. Elizabeth shouted for joy, "God has blessed you. You are the mother of God's Son!"

Playing Telephone

News travels fast. Sometimes it changes as it travels. Read the story "You Too?" Then read the talking telephones below. Cross out all the news that has changed.

"You will have many sons and daughters."

"God has blessed you."

"God's Holy Spirit will make it happen."

"You are the mother of God's Son!"

"I will do what my friends want."

"Your cousin Elizabeth can do anything."

"God can do just about anything."

Mary's Song

Mary — **time** — **angel** — **baby** — **people** — **down** — **God** — **song** — **happy**

Mary stayed at Elizabeth's house. She had time to think. The angel promised her a baby. Mary was engaged to Joseph. But she was not married. With a baby no man would marry her. She would not have a husband. People would look down on her. To be alone with God's baby? That would be very hard. Mary knew it was right to have God's baby. She sang a song of praise to God. Here is part of Mary's song. "I praise God. My heart is happy. I am not important. But God cares for me. God has done great things for me. God is holy. God is strong. God fills hungry people. God brings proud people down. God keeps promises forever." After 3 months Mary went home.

My Song

Make up a praise song like Mary's. What can you thank God for? What makes you happy? Put those things in your song. Write your song here.

My Song

God is . . .

Your name

Baby John

Elizabeth baby angel God Zechariah talk day name afraid

It was time for (Elizabeth) to have her (baby). Remember what the (angel) said? "You will have a son. You will name him John." Was the (angel) right? Was (Elizabeth)'s (baby) a boy? Yes! How good (God) was to (Elizabeth). Everyone was happy for (Elizabeth). (Zechariah) still could not (talk). On the 8th (day) an exciting thing happened. On the 8th (day) Jewish parents (name) their (baby). "What is his (name)?" people asked (Elizabeth). "His (name) is John," she said. No one believed (Elizabeth). "There are no Johns in the family," they said. So they asked (Zechariah). "What is his (name)?" (Zechariah) wrote, "His (name) is John." Suddenly (Zechariah) could (talk). He praised (God). The neighbors were (afraid). "What kind of (baby) is this?" they wondered.

Dot-to-Dot

Is counting from 1 to 89 easy for you? Then this dot-to-dot will be easy too. Draw lines to connect the dots. Color the picture. Use it to tell a story.

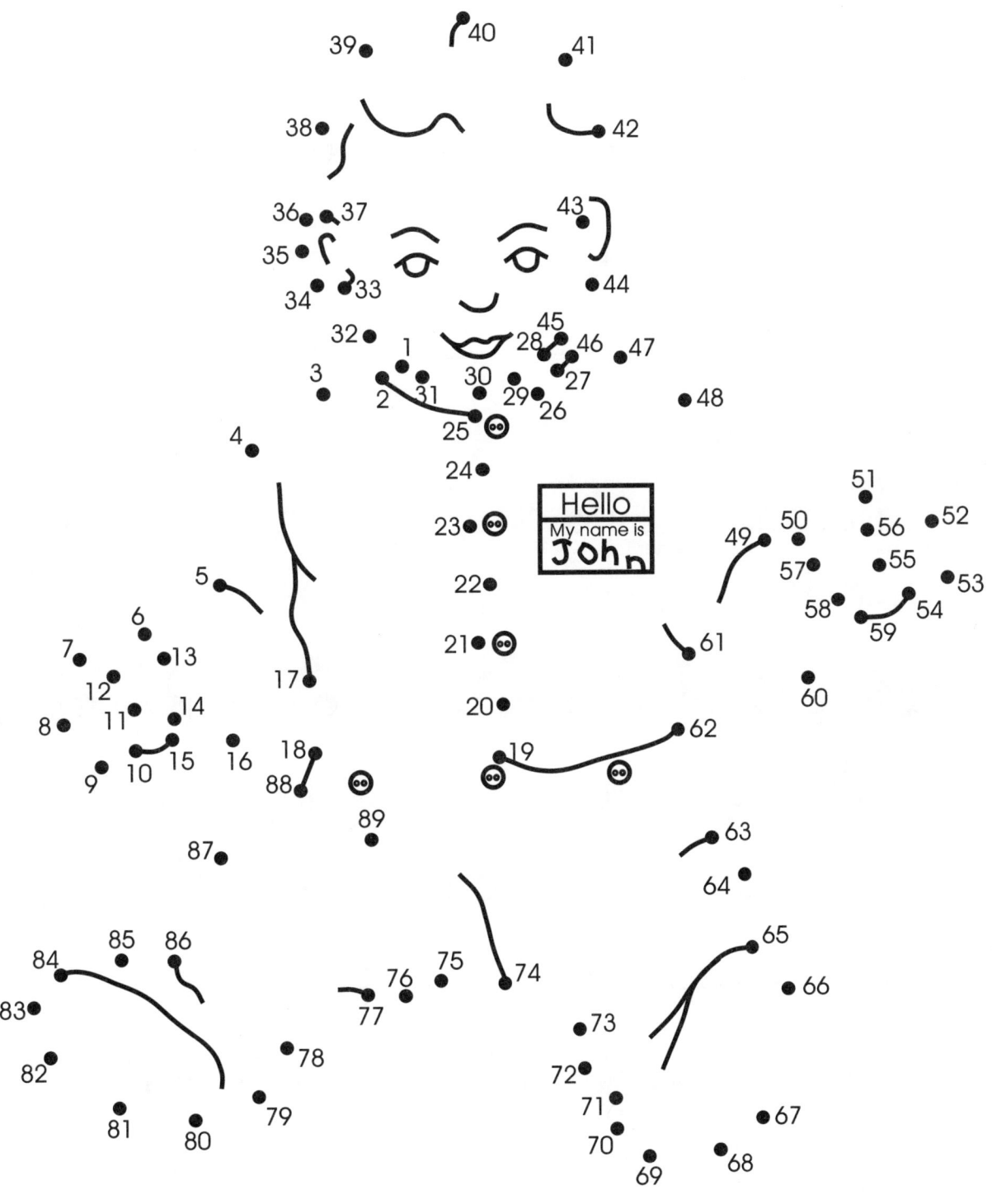

Baby Jesus

God · Mary · afraid · angel · baby · name · time · hospital · shepherd

God was good to Mary too. God wanted Joseph to marry her. But Joseph was afraid. Once again God sent an angel. "Joseph, do not be afraid to marry Mary," the angel said. "Her baby is God's Son. You will name him Jesus." Joseph obeyed God. Now Mary would have a husband. And a father for her baby. Later Mary and Joseph had to go on a trip. It came time for Mary's baby to be born. There were no rooms to rent. And no hospitals. So Mary had God's baby in an animal shelter. Angels sang the news to some shepherds. The shepherds came to see. They told Mary the angels' news. Mary put the news in her heart. In 8 days it was time to name the baby. What did they name him? Jesus.

Where's Who?

Read the stories "Baby John" and "Baby Jesus." Some of the names from these two stories are on this page. Search for them in the letters below. Circle them when you find them.

Find and circle the words here

JOHN
MARY
BABY
GOD

ELIZABETH
ZECHARIAH
SHEPHERDS
NEIGHBORS

JOSEPH
PARENTS
ANGEL
JESUS

```
            J O H N N
            S R E S E
            A H H H I
            N N T P G
            G E G E H
S H E P H E R D S B Y M H E G
P A T H N L B J O O R J A H L
S T N E R A P A J R E Z A R E
E I T P B N D O G S H I J E Y
B A B Y A A S U U S R N I E P
            E Z S A A
            R E I H M
            D H C L M
            S E A B E
            Z Y J O S
```

Lost!

Mary · baby · God · king · city · Lake Galilee · temple · teach · worry

Mary's baby was God's Son. God's Son was a king. King Herod heard about the new baby king. He gave a terrible order — "Kill all baby boys." So Mary and Joseph went on another trip. King Herod killed all the baby boys. But not Mary's. When it was safe, they went home. They lived in a city by Lake Galilee. Mary's Son grew. He was strong and wise. Once Mary and Joseph went to the temple in Jerusalem. Jesus was 12. On the way home Mary and Joseph looked around. No Jesus! Back to the temple they went. There was Jesus teaching the teachers! "We worried about you," Mary said. Jesus said, "Why do you worry? I am doing Father's work!" Who was his Father? God!

Cross Lines Maze

Mary and Joseph lost Jesus. Help them find Jesus. Draw a line through the maze from Mary to Jesus. Do not cross any black lines.

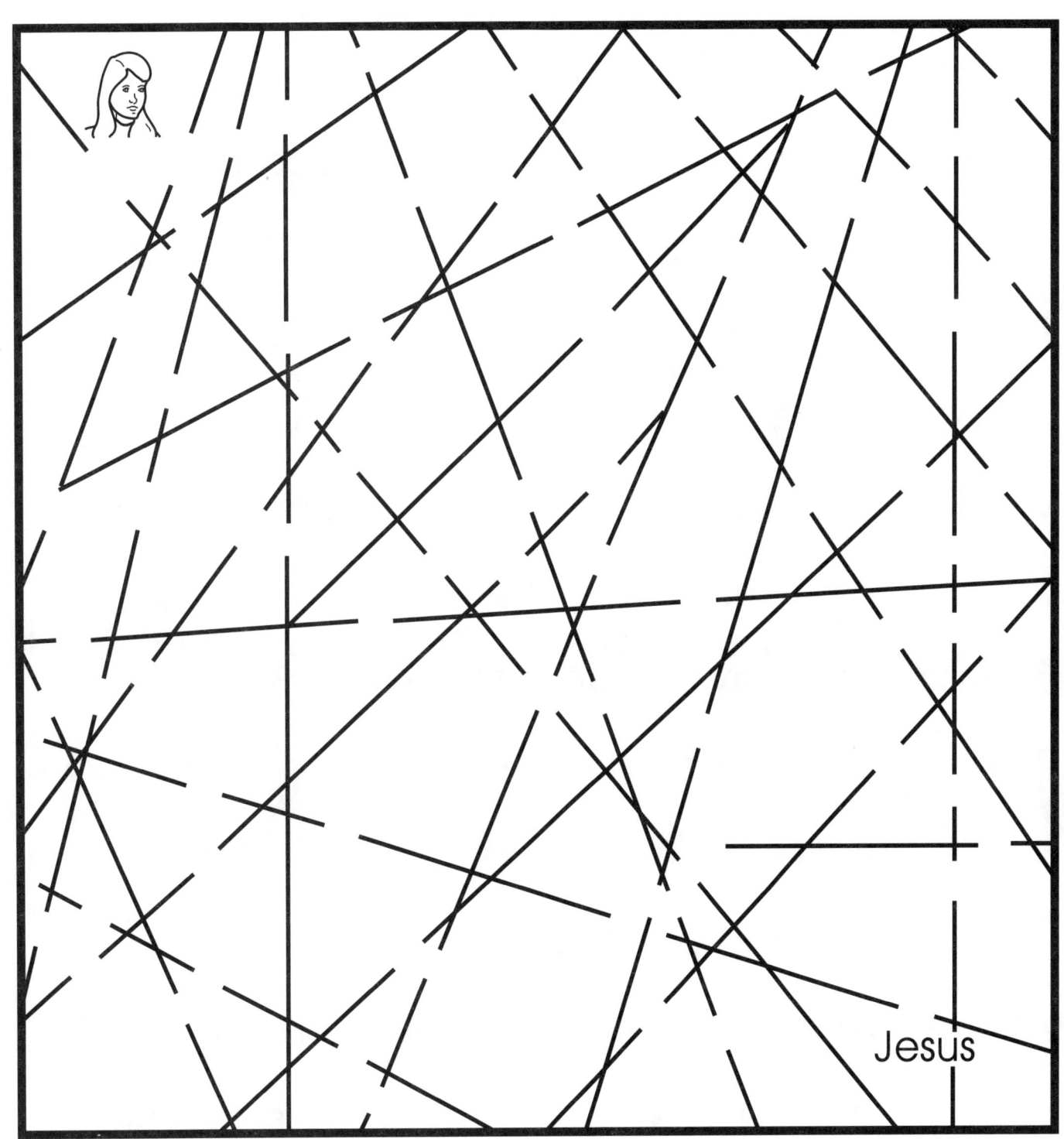

Boy Cousins Meet

Mary Jesus up Elizabeth desert locust preach dove voice

Mary's Son Jesus grew up. Elizabeth's son John grew up. They were good sons. The boy cousins became men. John lived in the desert. He ate locusts and honey. John was a preacher. "Get ready," he preached. "The Lord is coming. Change your hearts. Be baptized," he preached. "Are you the Lord?" people asked John. "No," John said. "He is much greater than I." One day Jesus came to John. "Baptize me," Jesus said. So John baptized Jesus, the Lord. The Holy Spirit came like a dove. The dove sat on Jesus' head. A voice from Heaven said, "You are my Son. I love you." Were Elizabeth and Mary there that day? We don't know. But Elizabeth and Mary knew that Jesus was the Lord.

What's Missing?

John ate locusts and wild honey. The locust in the center of the page is correct. All the others are missing something. Draw in the missing parts.

Color us!

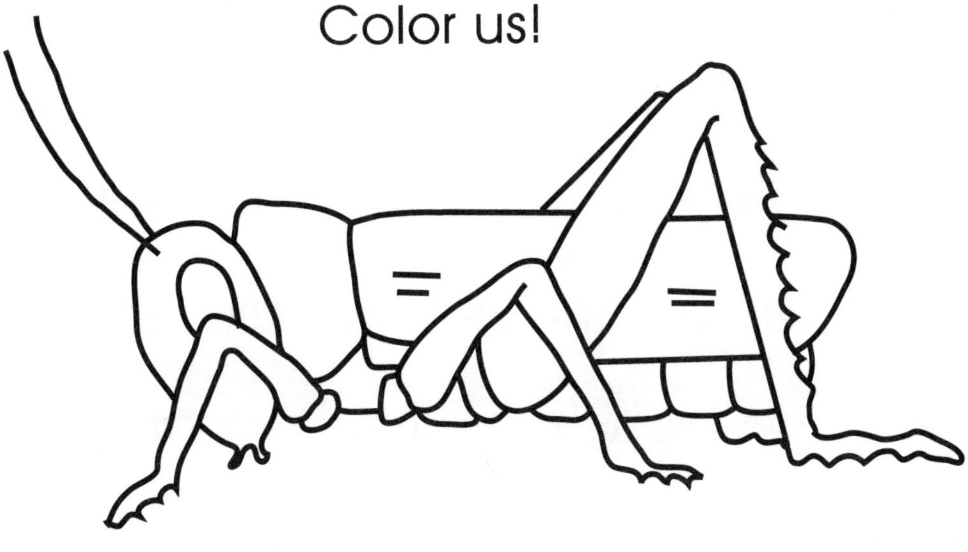

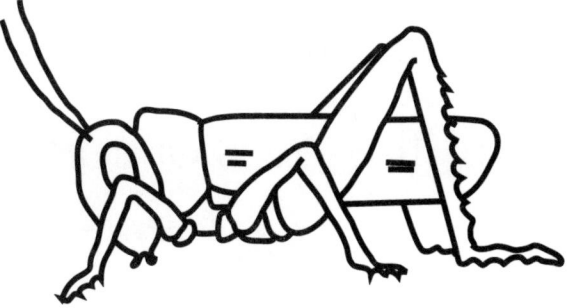

Wedding Party

Mary Jesus wedding feast wine help jar can up

Mary and her Son Jesus went to a wedding feast. There was food and wine at the wedding feast. Soon the wine was all gone. This was not good! Mary knew Jesus was God's Son. She knew he could help. Mary said to the servants at the feast, "Do what Jesus tells you to do." There were 6 jars as big as trash cans. "Fill these jars with water," Jesus said. The servants did what Jesus said. They filled up the big jars. "Now serve the master of the feast," Jesus said. The servants took water from the jars to the master. He took a drink of ... not water, but good wine! "You saved the best wine for last," the master said to the groom! Jesus had turned the water into wine. It was a miracle!

What Doesn't Belong?

Read the story "Wedding Party." Some of the pictures below belong to the story. Color them. Some of them do not belong. Cross them out.

On a Plate

God   Elizabeth   love   Bible   king   jail   party   dance   plate

 chose  to raise John.  taught John to  and obey . The doesn't say what happened to . But it does say what happened to 's son. Many people thought John was strange. They did not like him.  Herod's wife hated John.  Herod put John in . The 's wife wanted John to die. One day she found a way. It was  Herod's birthday. There was a big . The 's daughter d at the .  Herod liked her . "I will give you anything," he said. "I want John's head on a ," she said. Off came John's head!  would have been sad. But 's work for 's son was done.

Filling in for John

The words on this page are from the story "On a Plate." Fill them into the empty boxes. Two letters are filled in to help you get started.

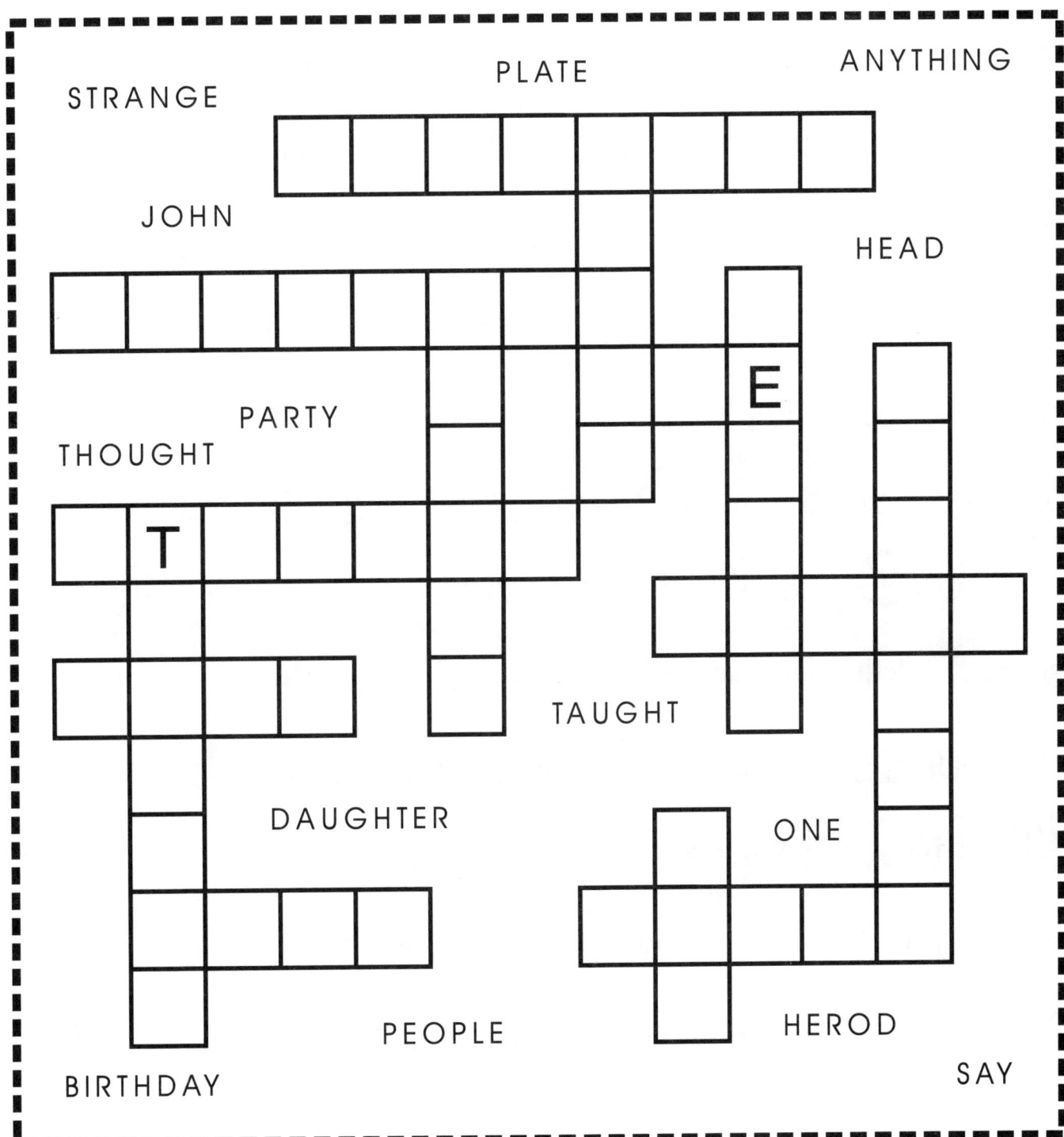

On a Cross

God | Mary | Jesus | sin | Jew | cross | king | sad | earth

God chose Mary to raise Jesus. She taught God's Son Jesus to love and obey God. The Bible does not say much about Mary after Jesus grew up. But we know about Mary's Son. Jesus taught about God. And love. He healed sick people. Jesus said, "Change your hearts. Stop your sin. God will forgive you." Jesus did not sin. Still many Jews hated him. "Take him away! Kill him on a cross!" the Jews shouted. "Will you kill your king?" the Jews' leader asked. "Jesus is not our king," they shouted. So they killed Jesus on a cross. Mary stood by the cross. How sad Mary must have felt! Her Son's work on earth was done. But the cousins had changed the world forever!

True-False Test

First read all the stories in this book. Then read each sentence below. If a sentence is true, put an X in the True box. If it is not true, put an X in the False box.

	True	False
1. 👩 came from a family of 👑s.	☐	☐
2. 👩 ♡d and obeyed ☁GOD.	☐	☐
3. 👩's 🎵 showed how ☹ she was.	☐	☐
4. 👩 said, "His 🏷Ben is 👨."	☐	☐
5. 👩's 👶 was born in a ✚.	☐	☐
6. 👩 found 👨 📖ing in the 🏛.	☐	☐
7. 👩's son never grew ⬆.	☐	☐
8. 👨 and 👩 went to a 💍 together.	☐	☐
9. 👩 taught John to ♡ ☁GOD.	☐	☐
10. 👩 stood by the ✝ when 👨 died.	☐	☐

Answers

Playing Telephone
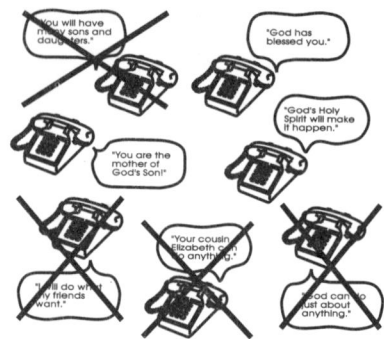

Dot-to-Dot

Where's Who?
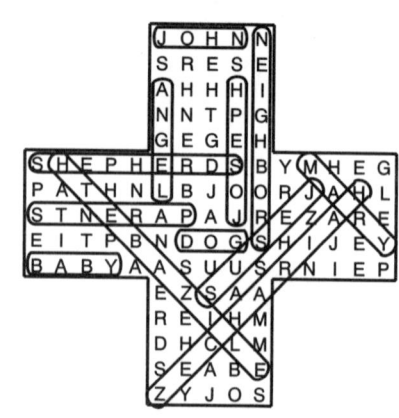

Cross Lines Maze

What Doesn't Belong?

Filling in for John
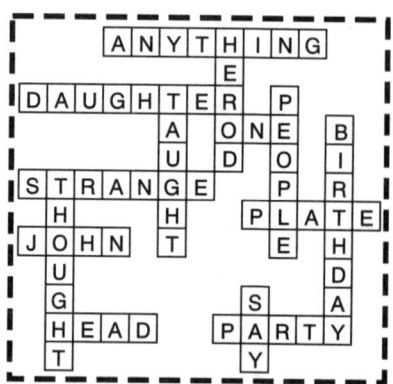

Adding Angels: There are 18 angels.

Picture Spelling: "You will give birth to a son, and you will name him Jesus. He will be great." Luke 1:31, 32

What's Missing?: One locust is missing its back leg.   One is missing the eye.   One is missing its antenna.   And one is missing its body.

True-False Test: 1-true, 2-true, 3-false, 4-false, 5-false, 6-true, 7-false, 8-false, 9-true, 10-true